#MTALEO

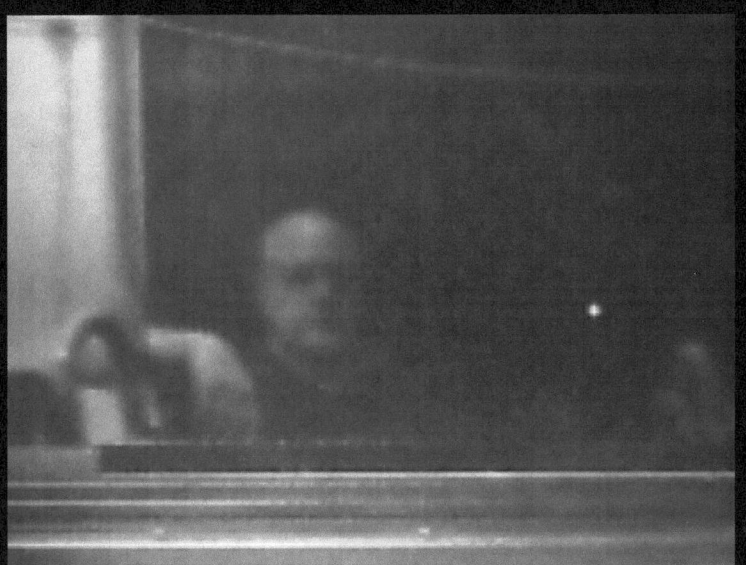

Adventures in Mass Transit

Leo Soderman - Words and Images

Thanks to all who encouraged me to produce this book. I hope it's enjoyed.

- Leo

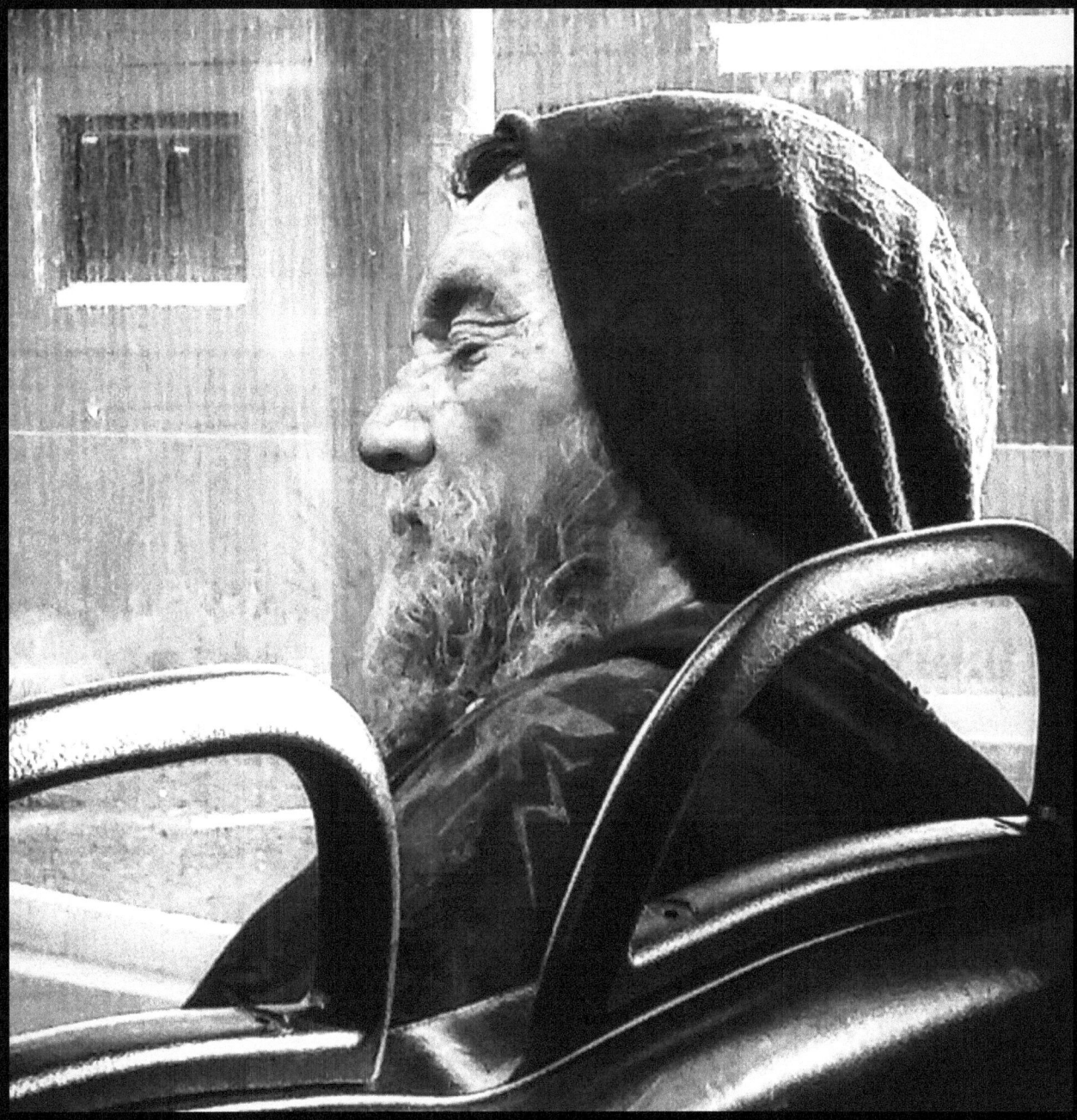

In the summer of 2014, I got the "fortunate" experience of needing to start taking mass transit to get to work. My daily commute of 35-45 minutes became a 3-hour adventure - each way.

As I rode bike, rail and bus, I initially just tried to sink into a corner and ignore everything around me. But as time passed, I grew more comfortable and started noticing things around me.

Some of what I saw made me laugh. Others made me want to cry.

I hope you enjoy these images and anecdotes and a look at what my daily Mass Transit Adventures have been like.

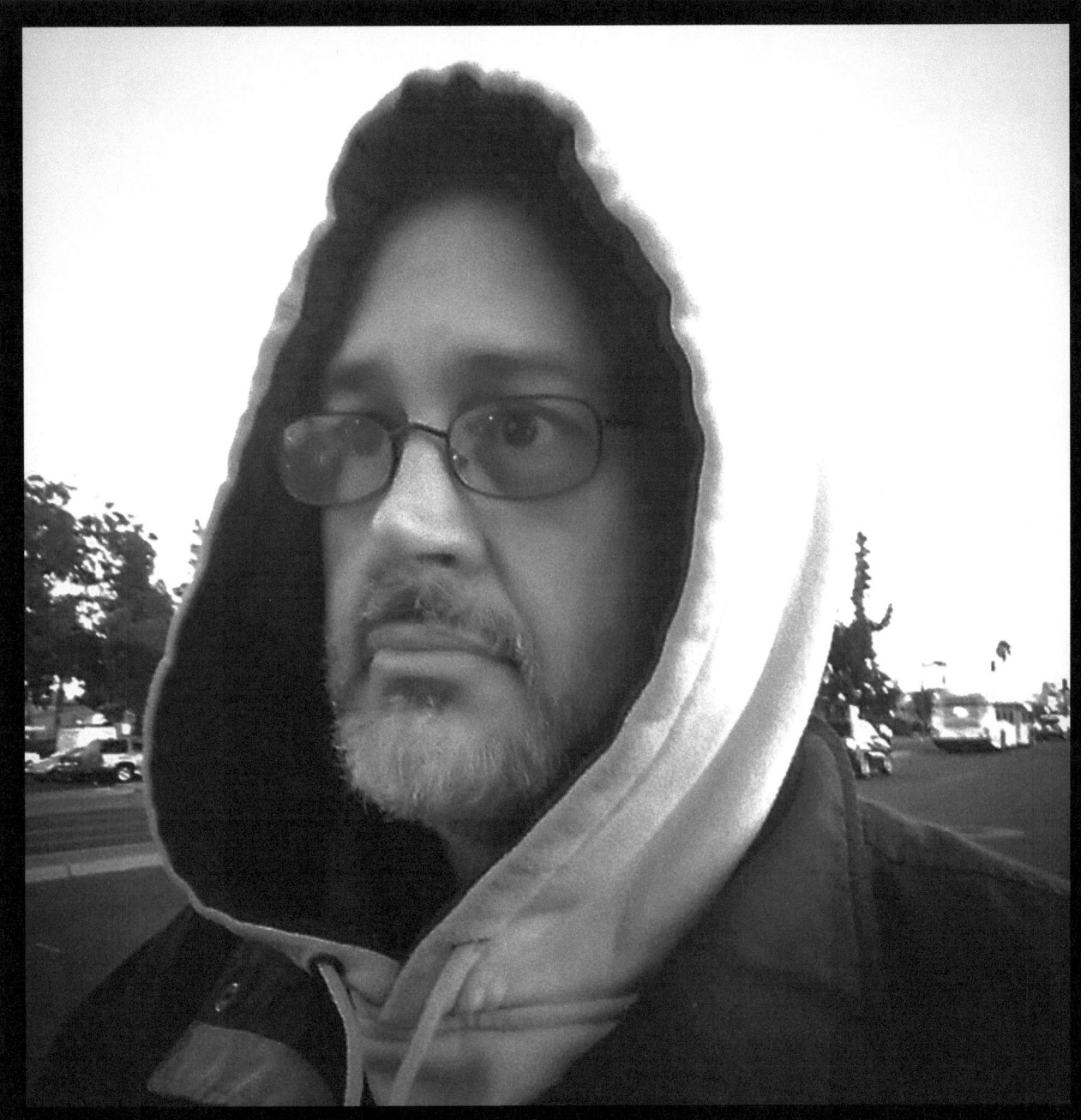

Some mornings, the opportunity to have a laugh is ripe. Like the day this woman got on the bus and sat directly across from me. "To hell with your mountains" it says.

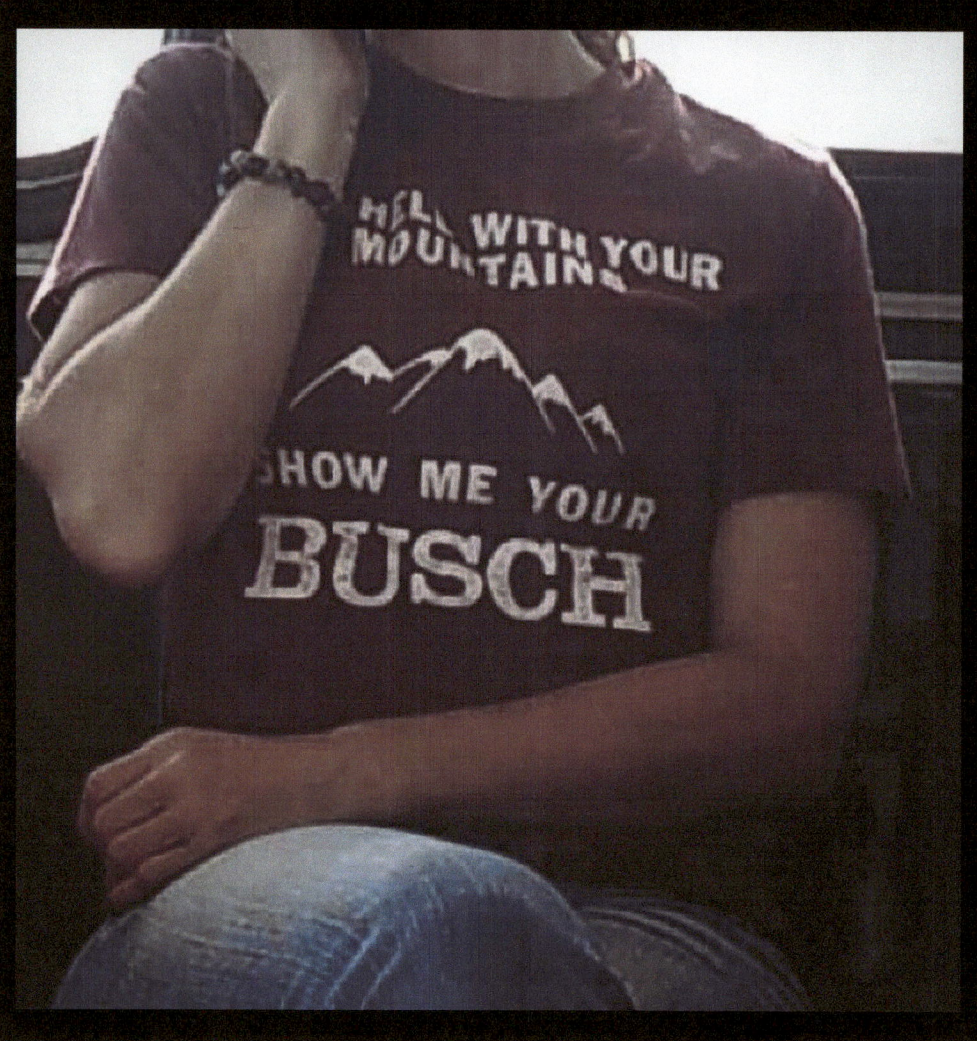

After going through the experience of my wife's pregnancy before my daughter was born, I totally get this shirt. And she wasn't really even showing yet....

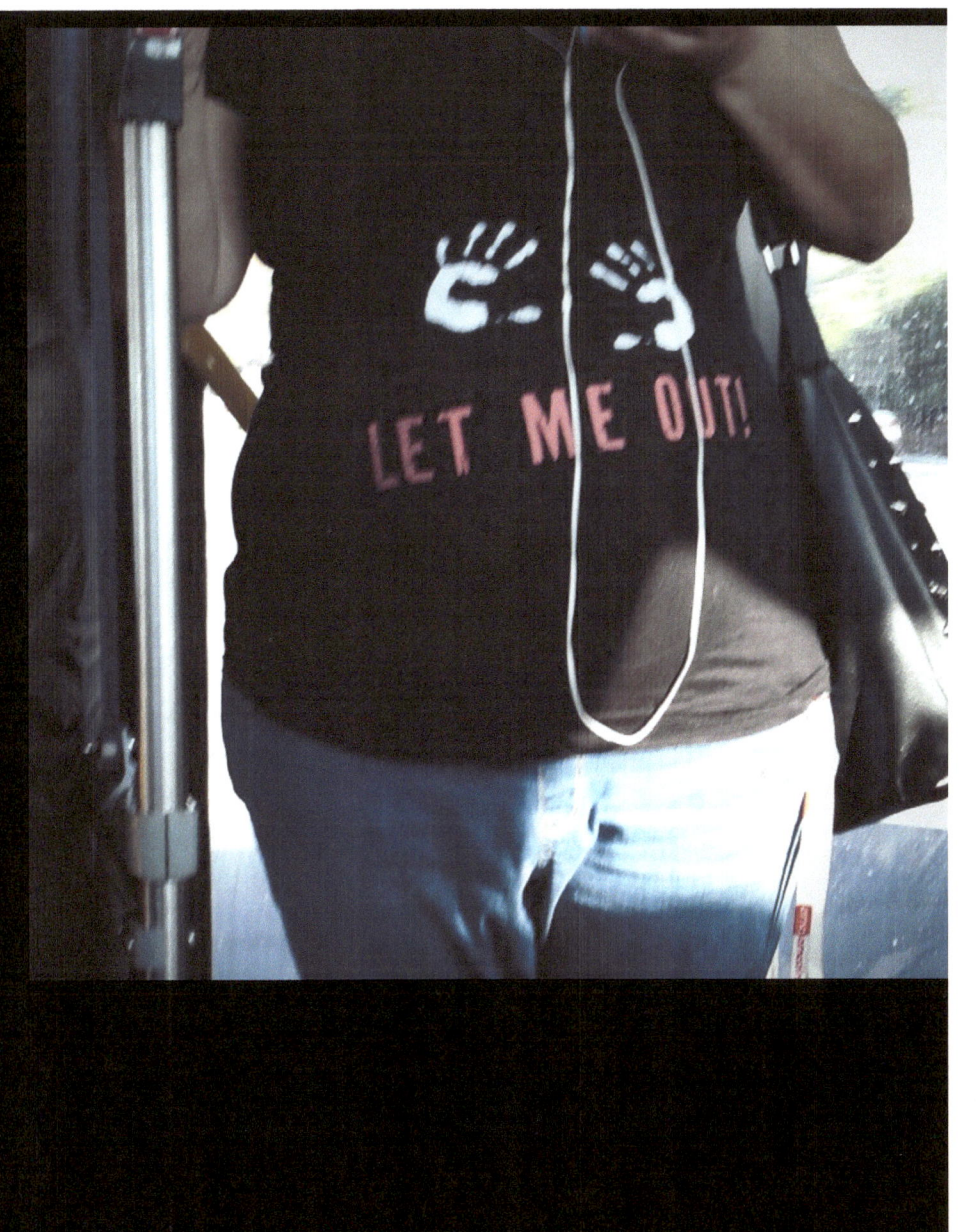

Other days, it's harder to smile. Some of the folks I see on the ride look completely lost, as if they've lost hope in ever seeing a better day.

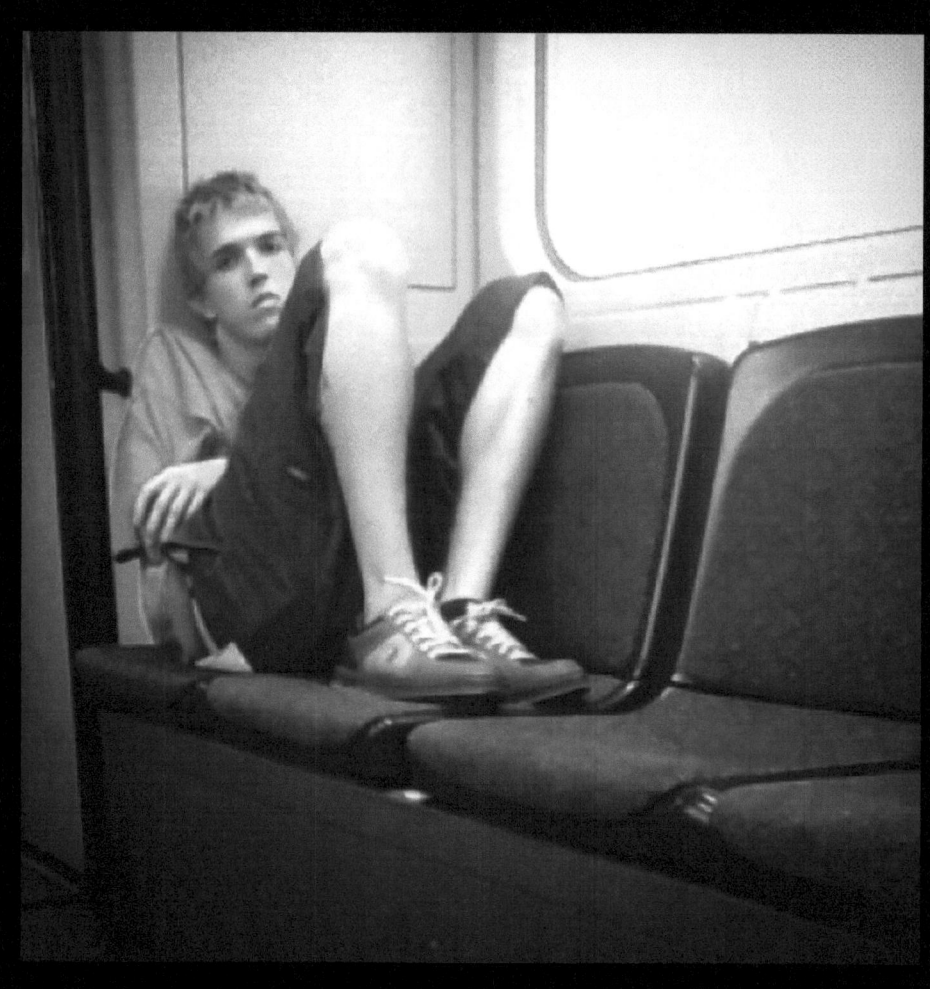

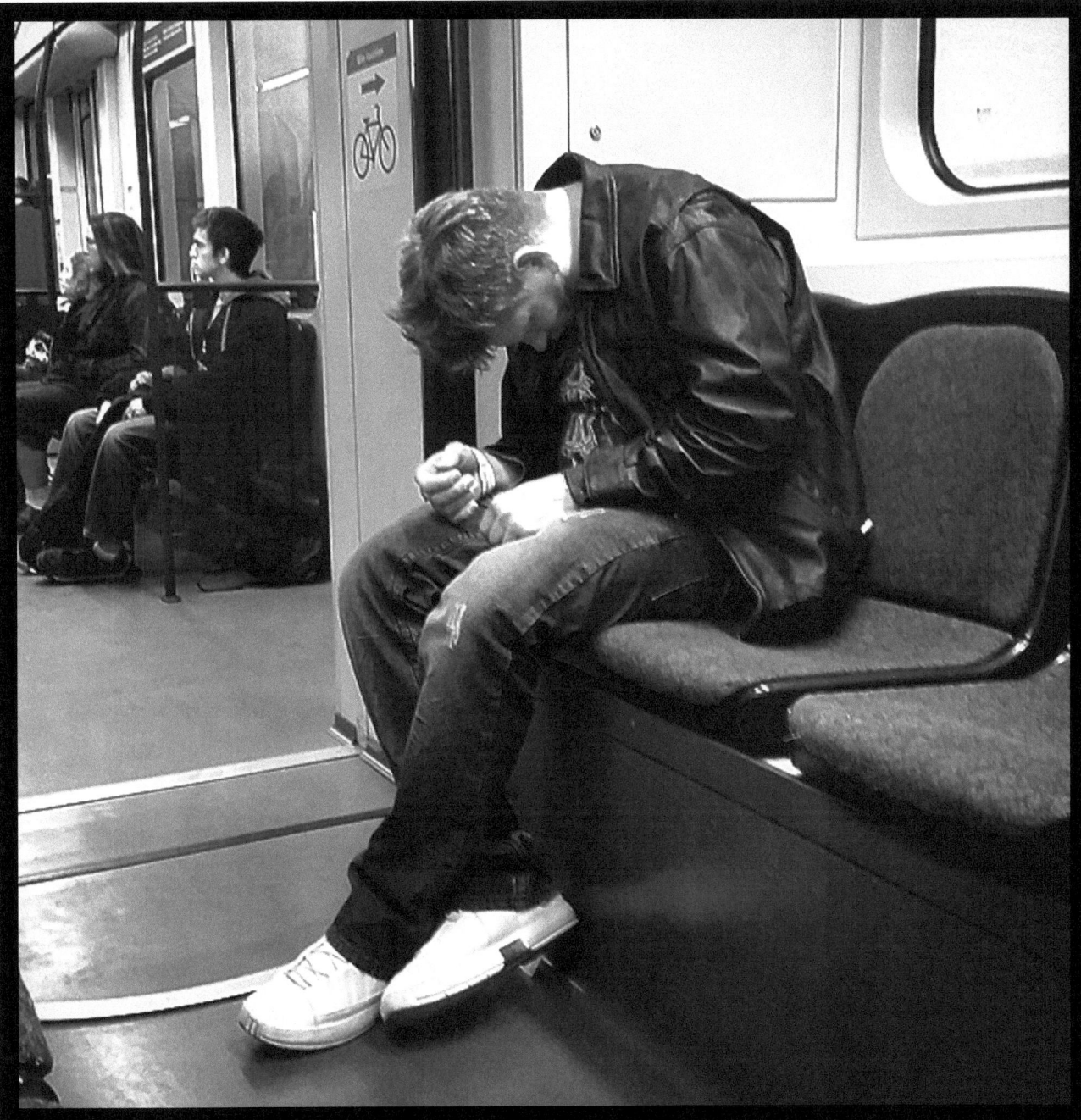

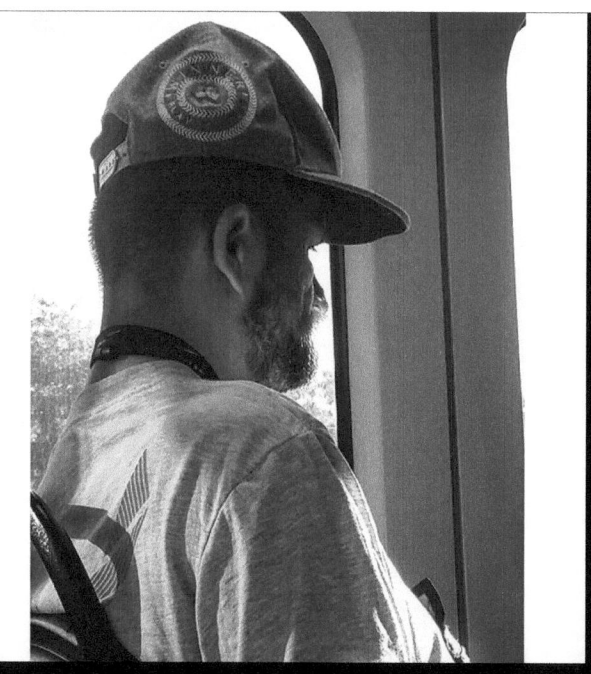

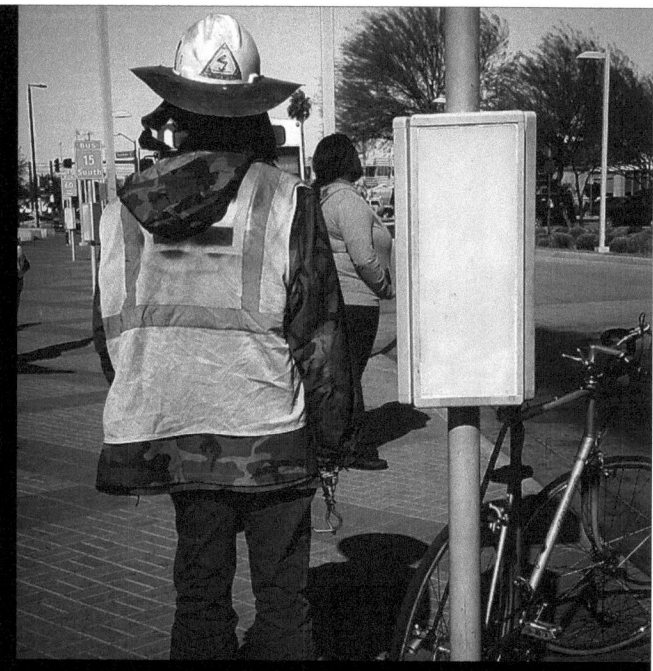

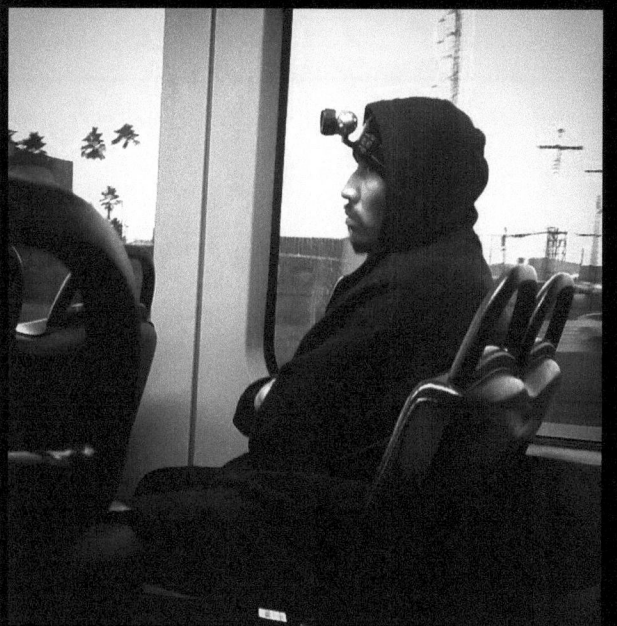

HEADGEAR

Top left: Conehead cap

Top right: Golden Helmet of Mambrino

Bottom left: One headlight

Opposite page: Monkey on your head?

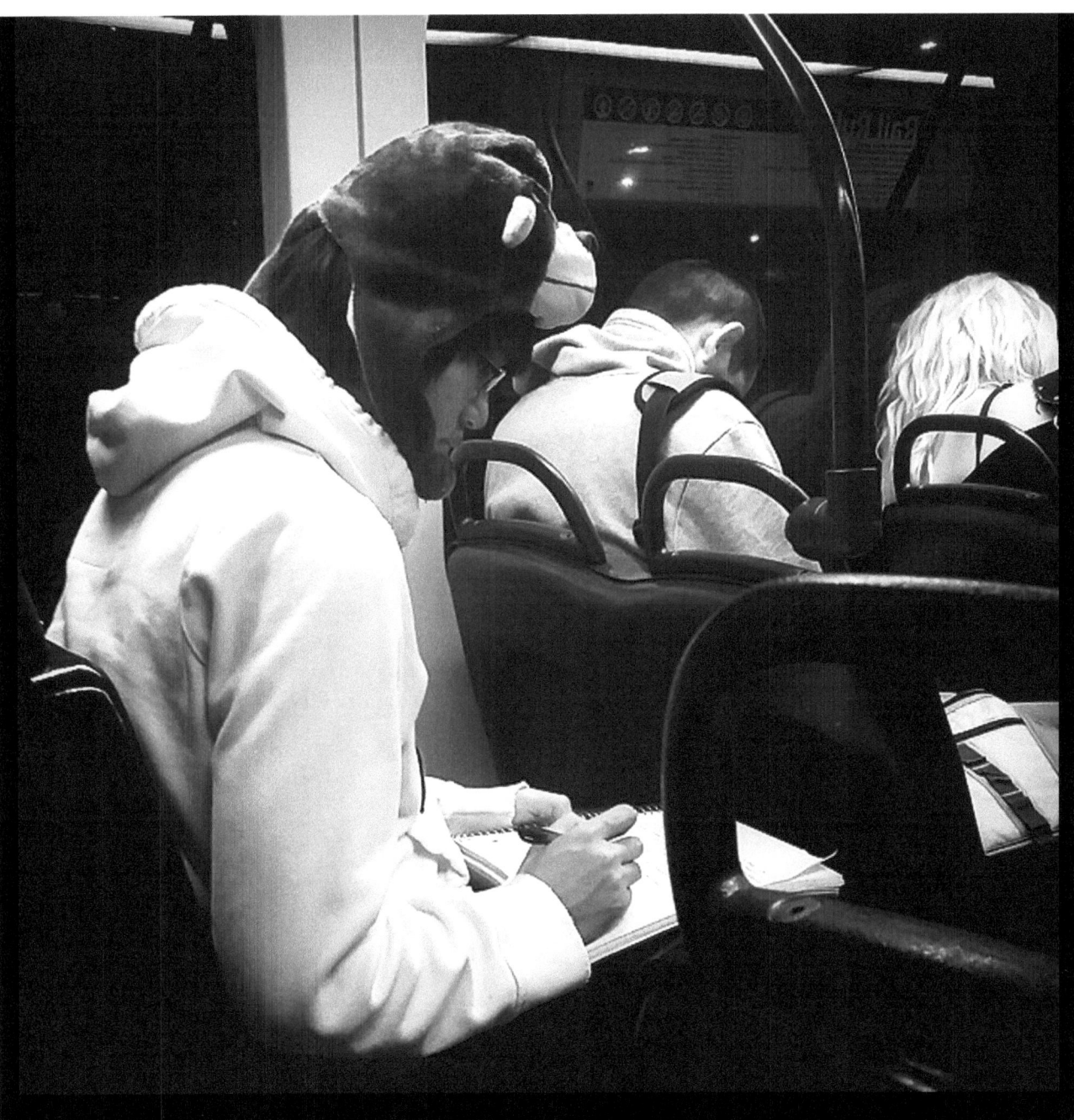

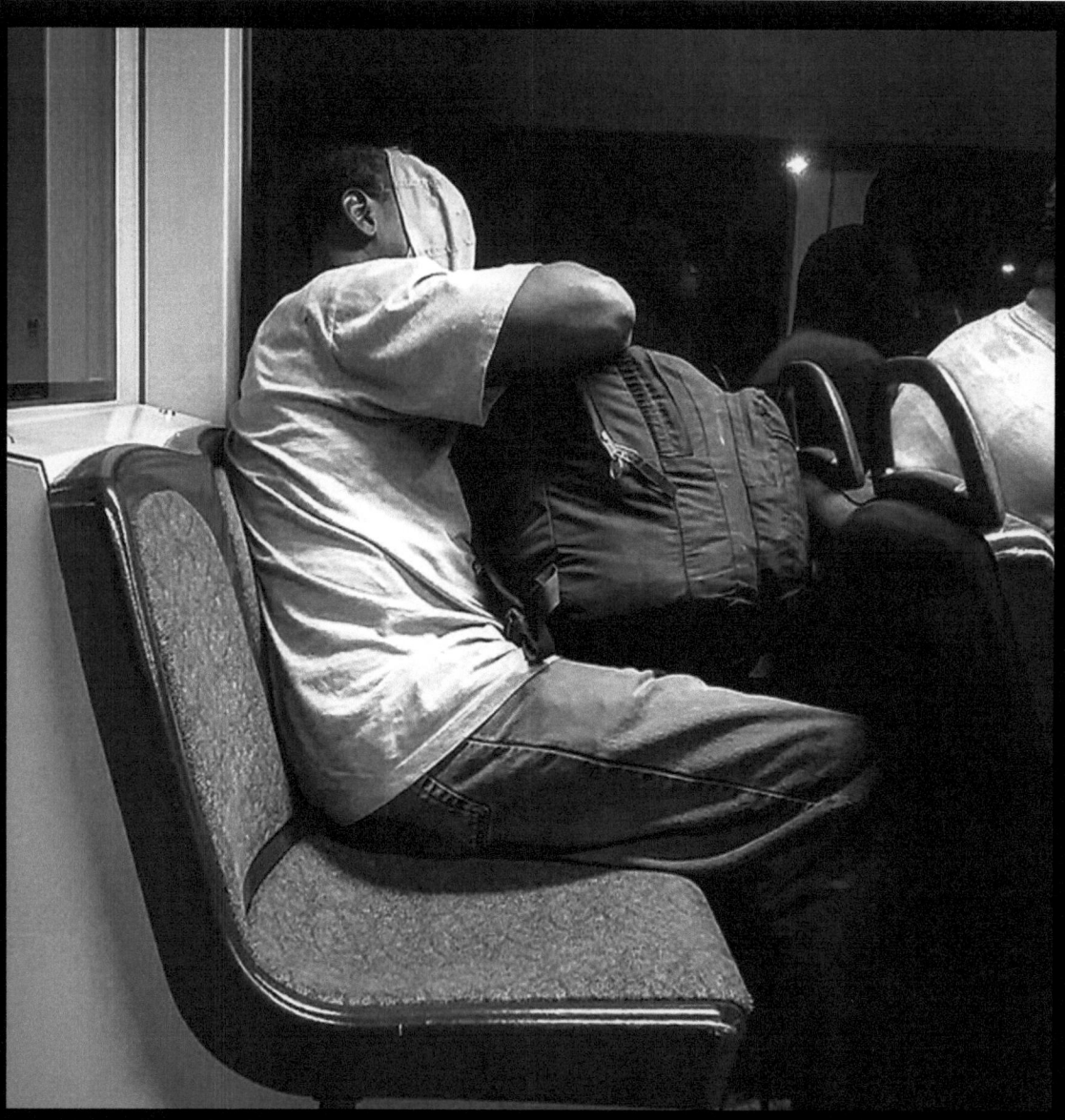

His hat is eating his face

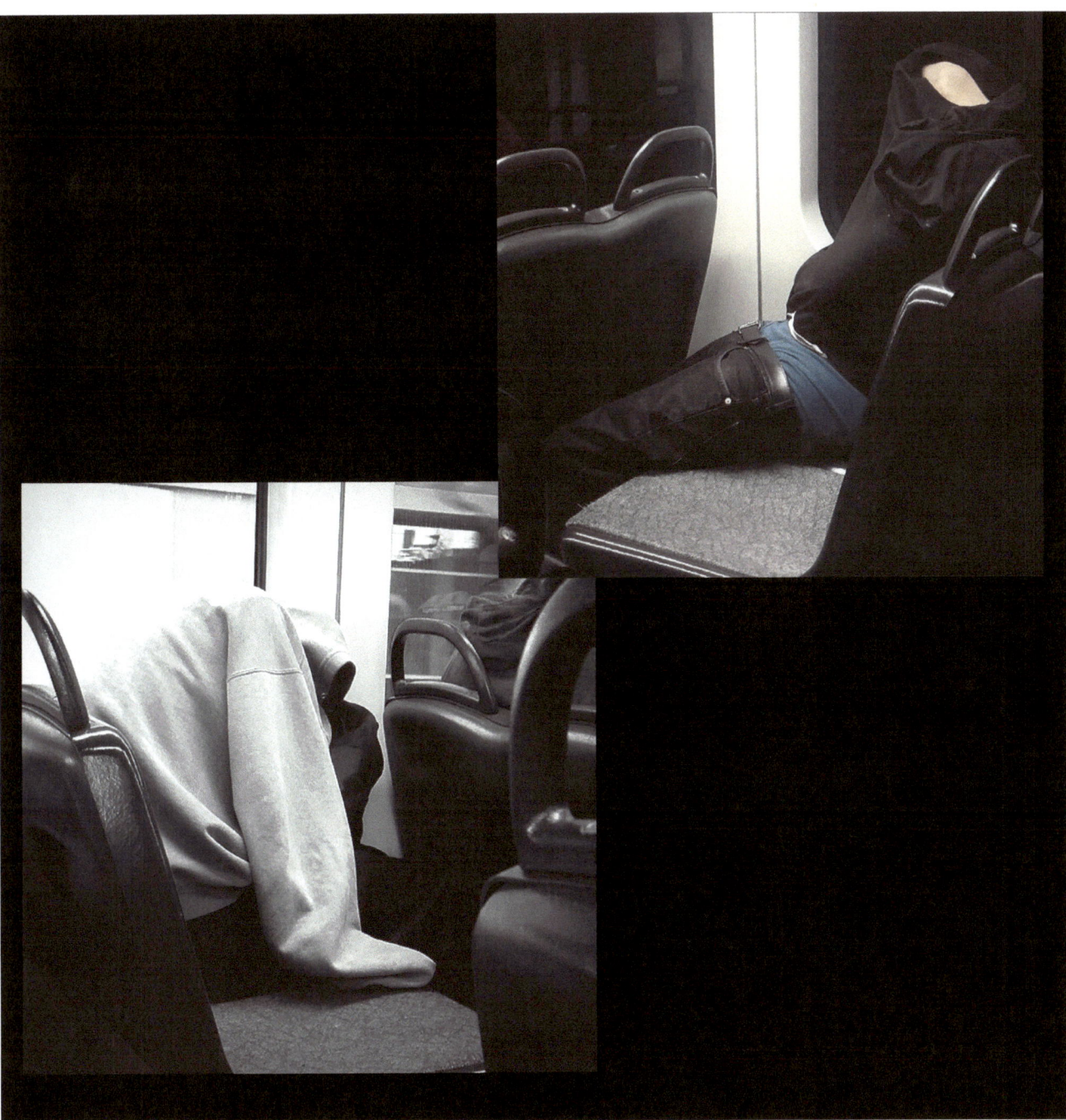

Building Materials

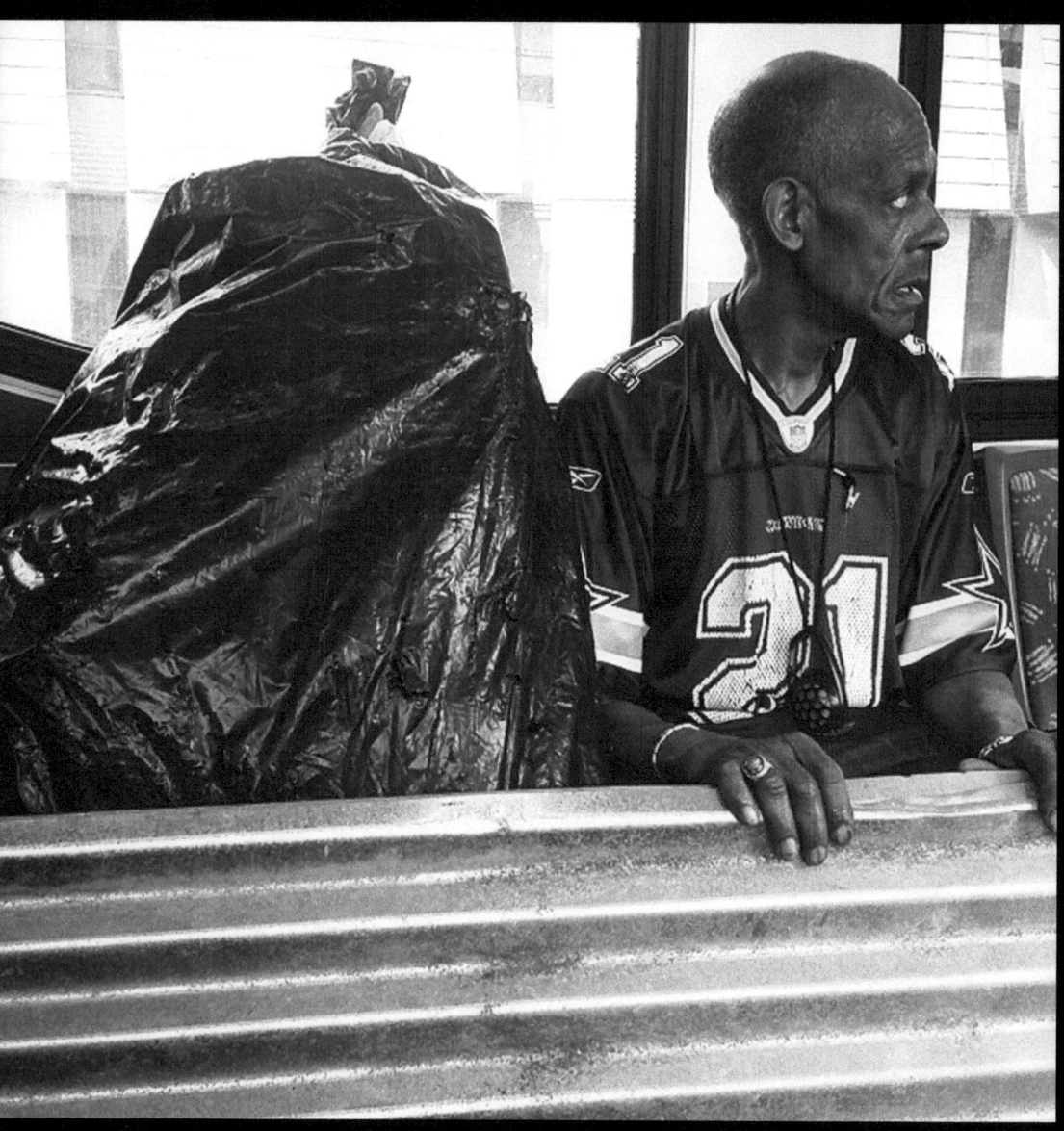

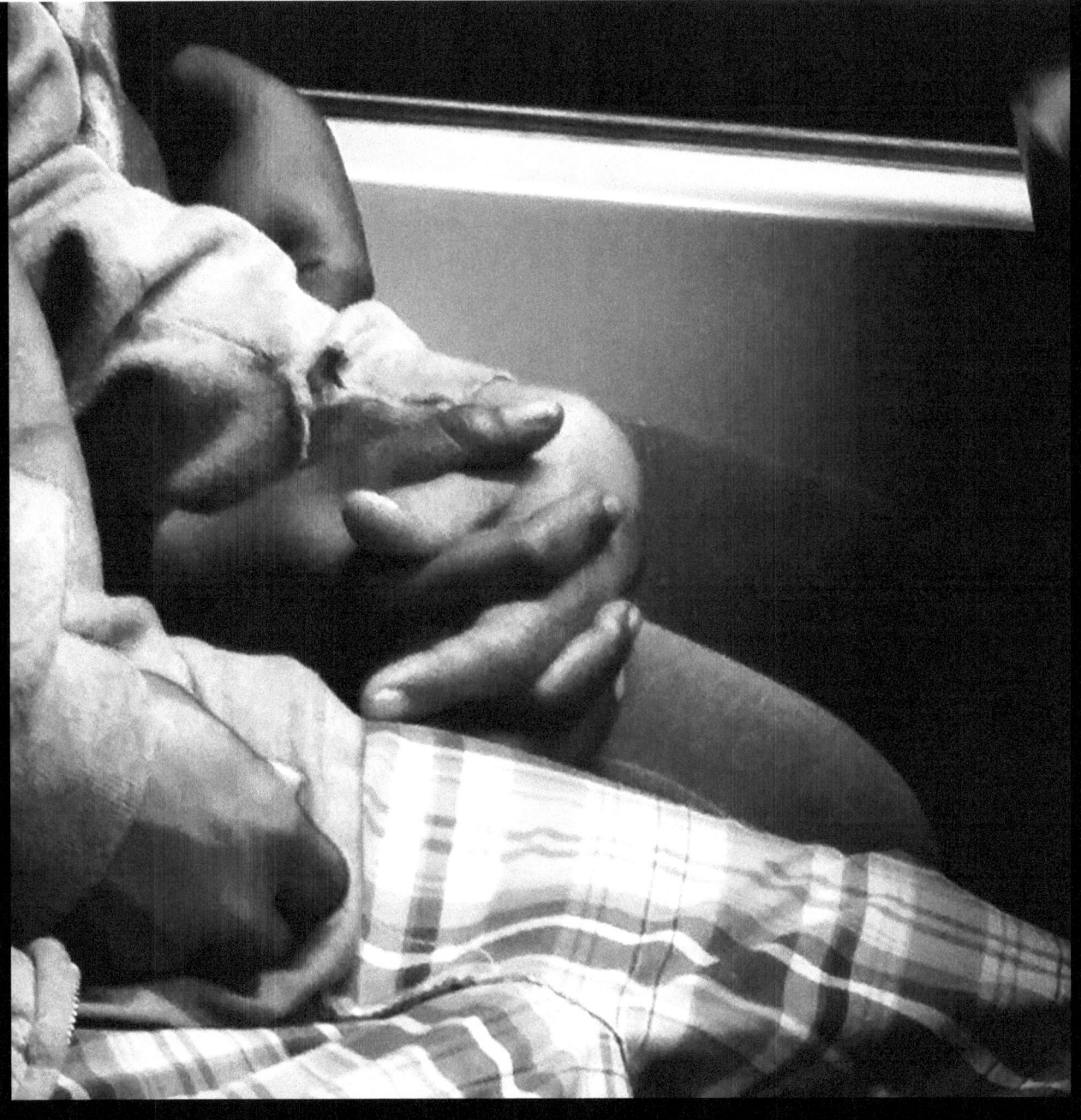

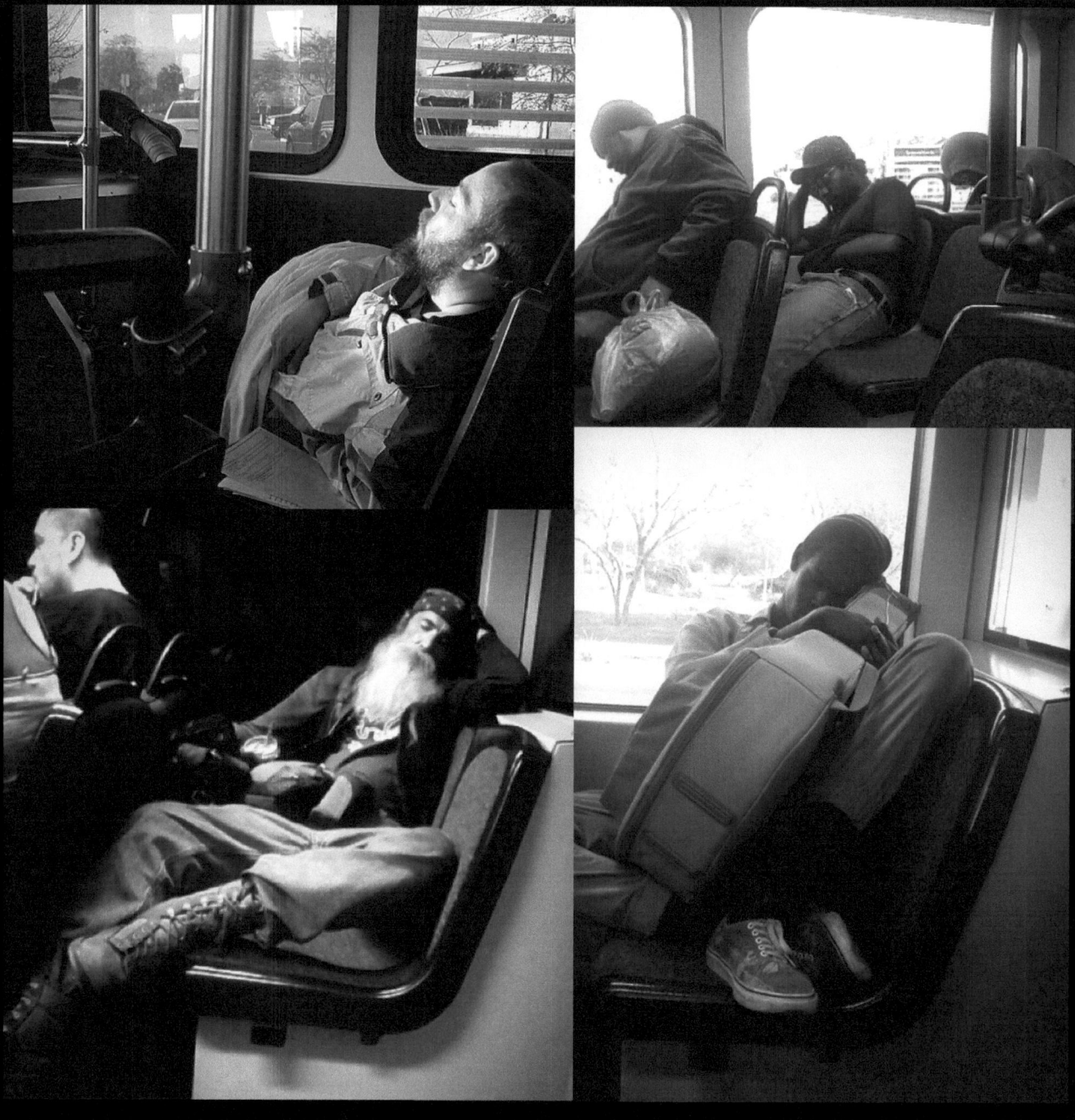

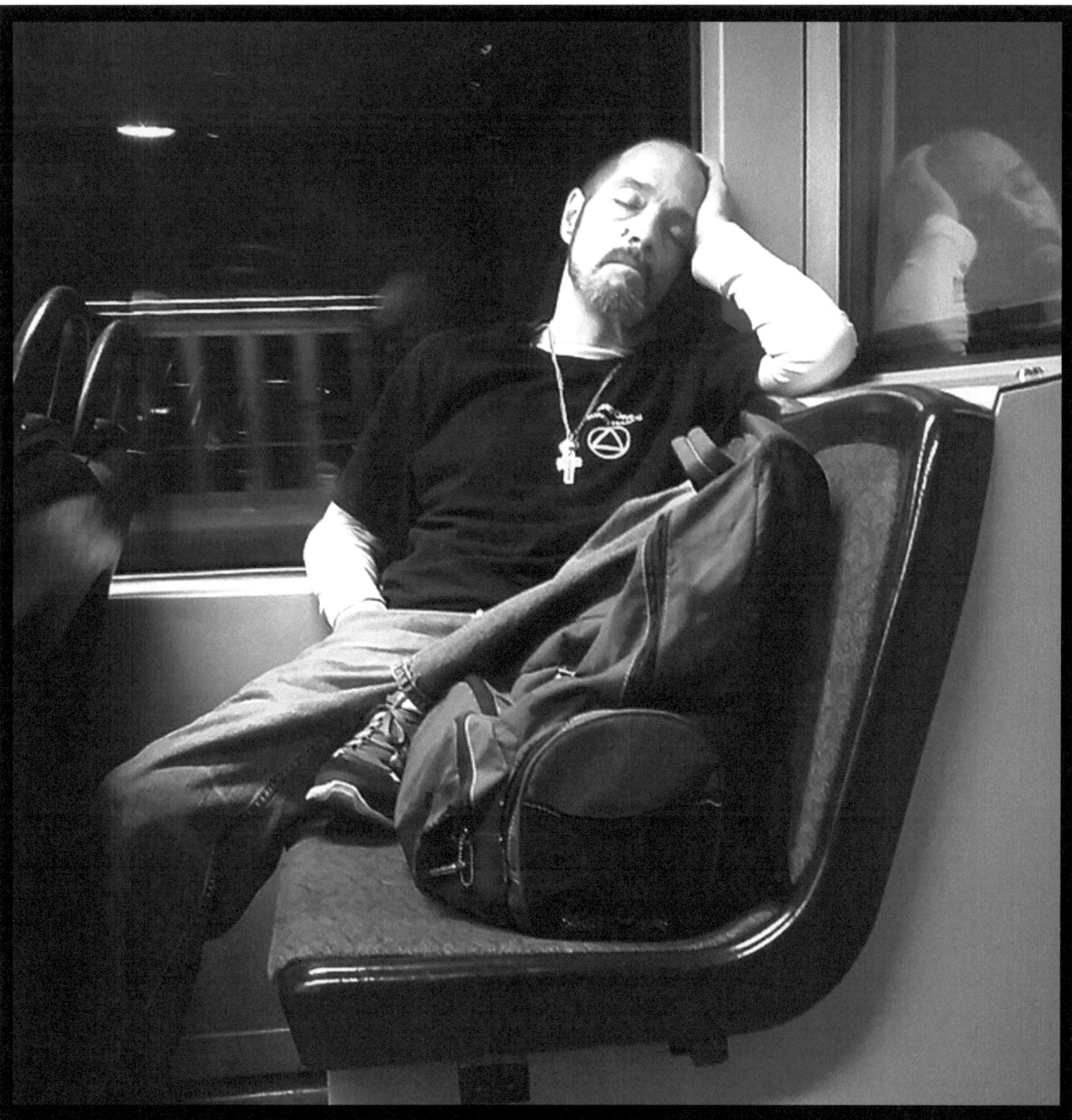

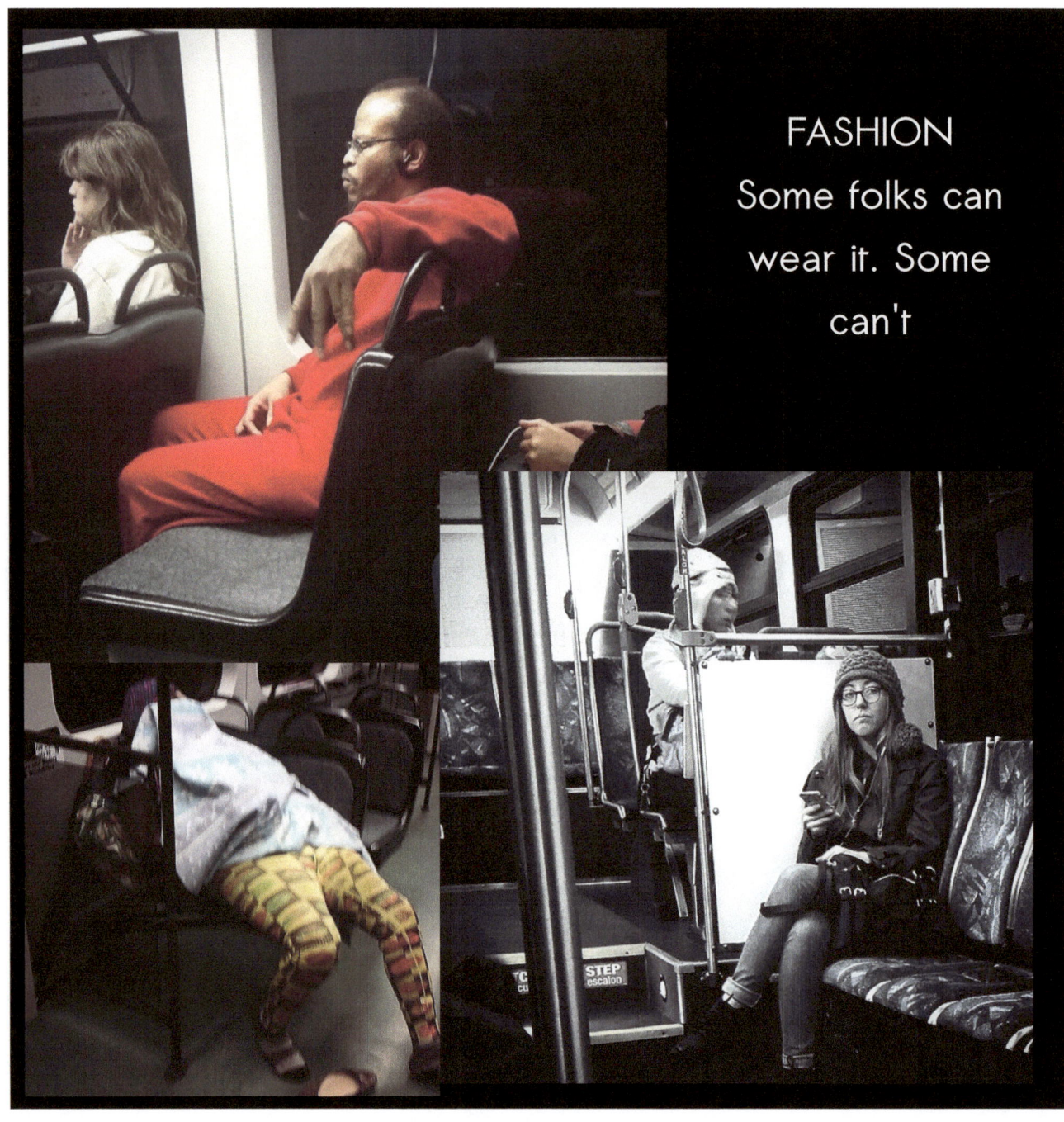

FASHION
Some folks can
wear it. Some
can't

This should not be
a hairstyle.

Either a lot of time in the
tanning booth, or Williy
Wonka's missing an
employee.

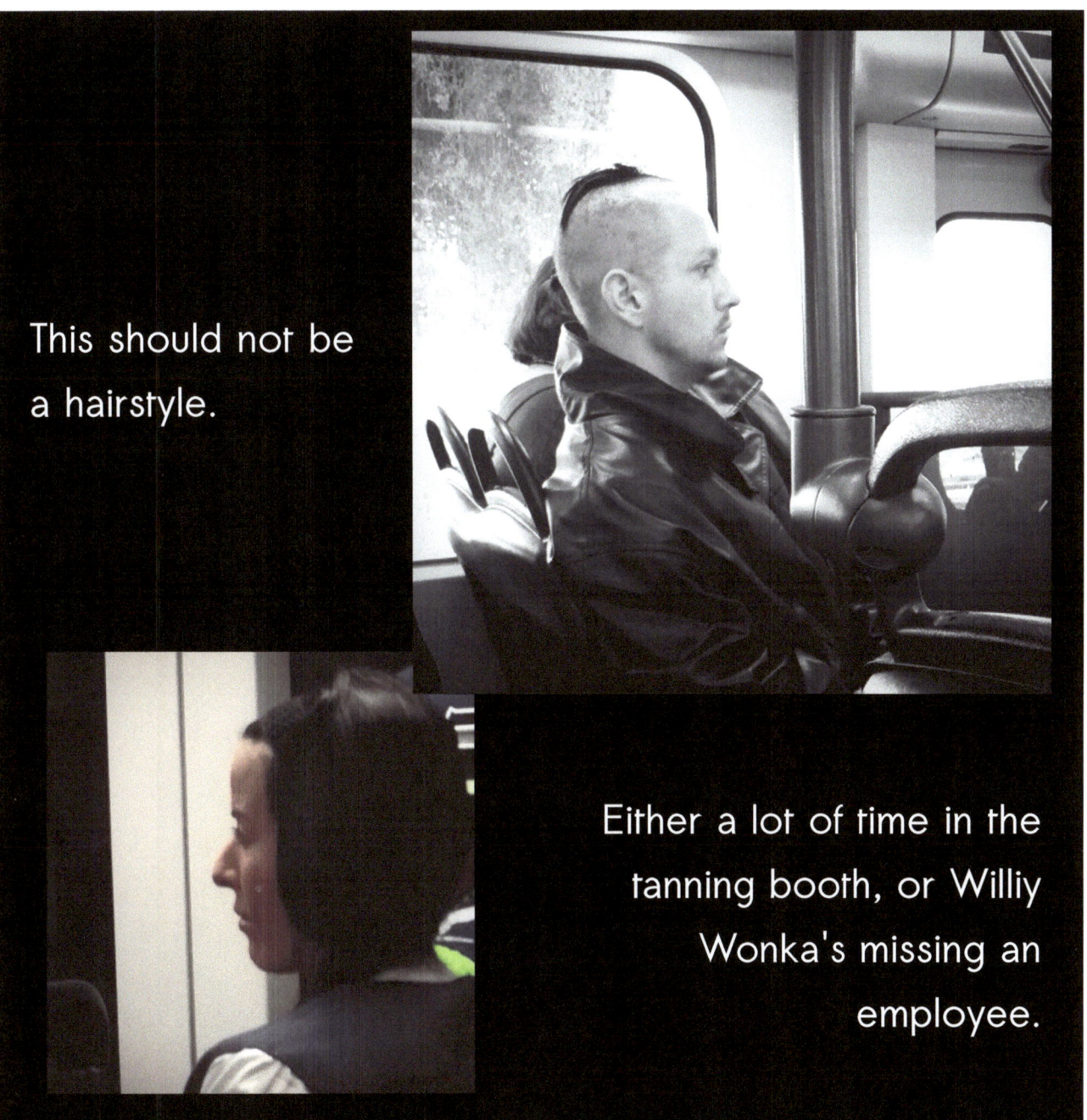

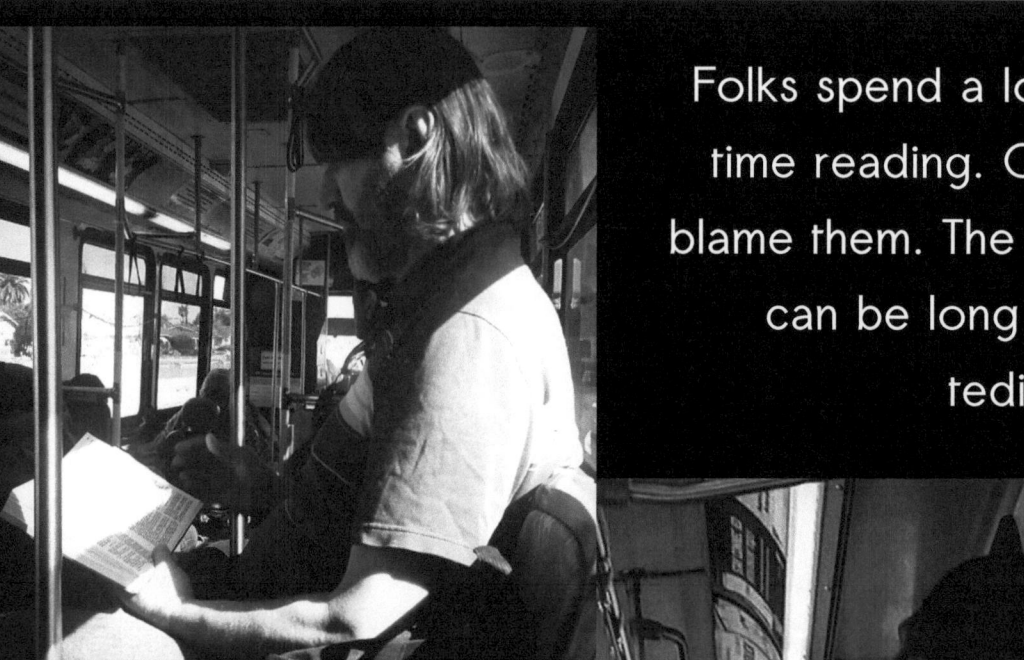

Folks spend a lot of time reading. Can't blame them. The ride can be long and tedious.

This gentleman was reading the good book. But his eyesight was so poor that he had to hold it just inches from his nose.

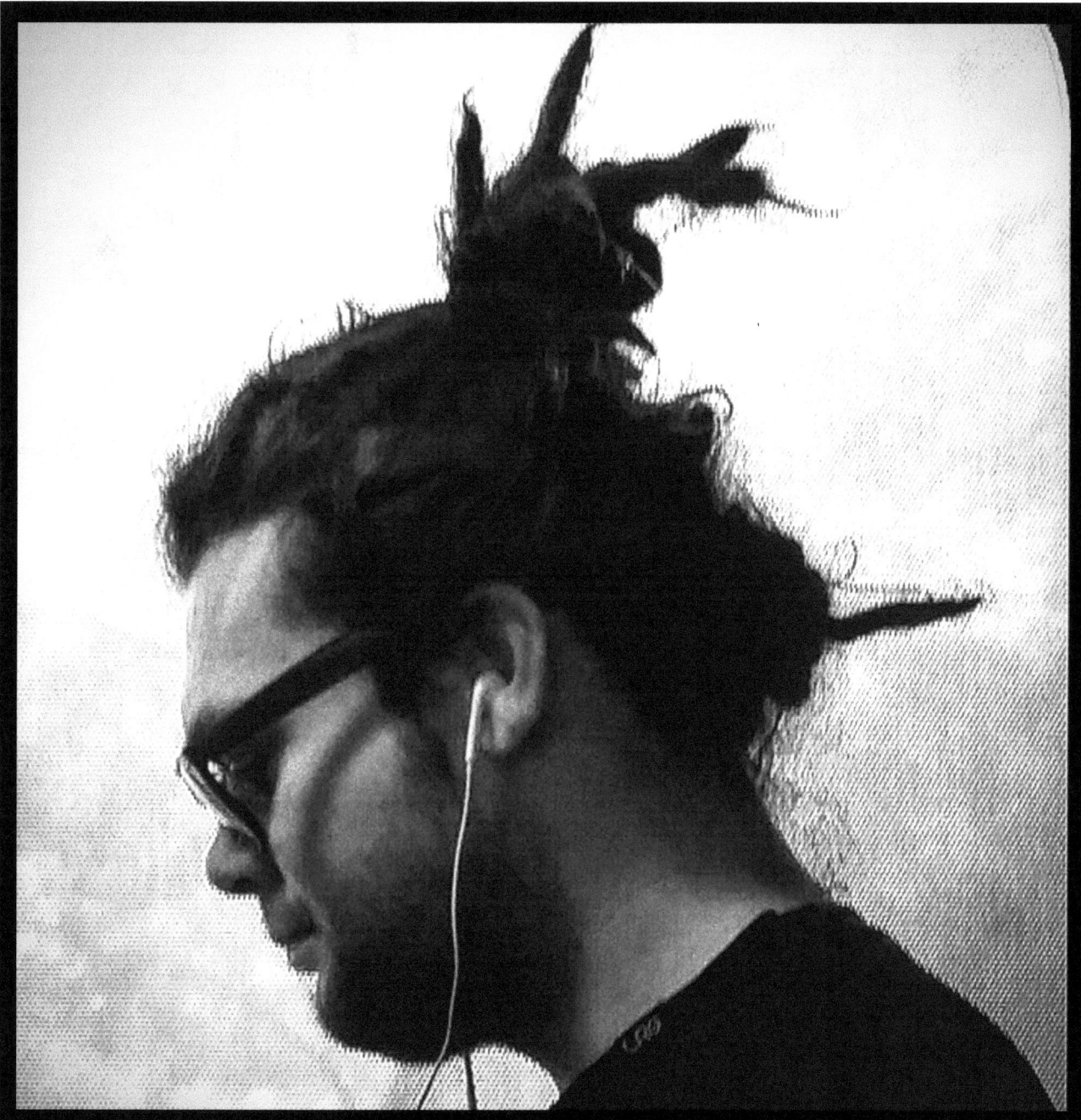

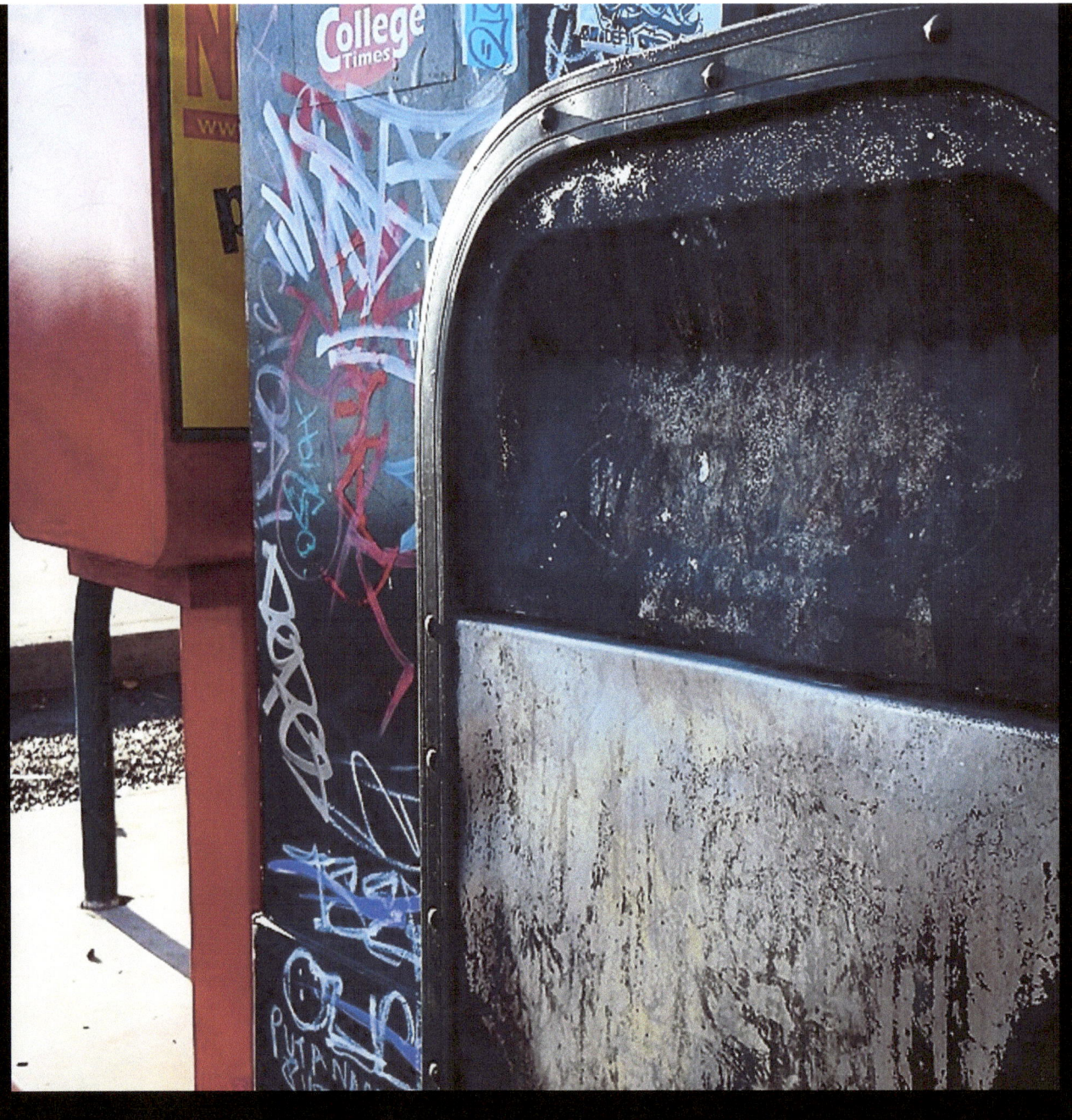

Note the beltline. Exactly what is the point?

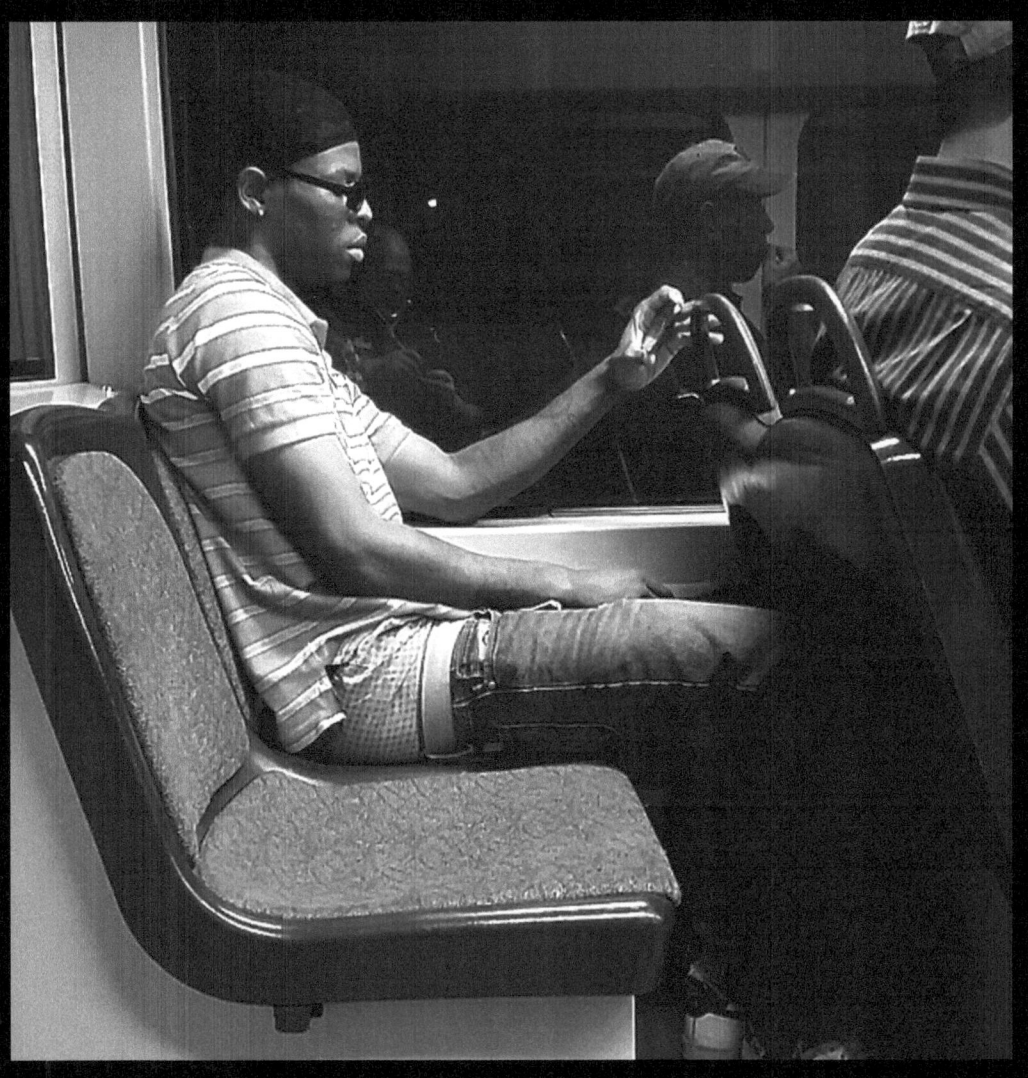

This gentleman was dancing around carrying a tree branch just before he sat down and I snapped this pic. Primal.

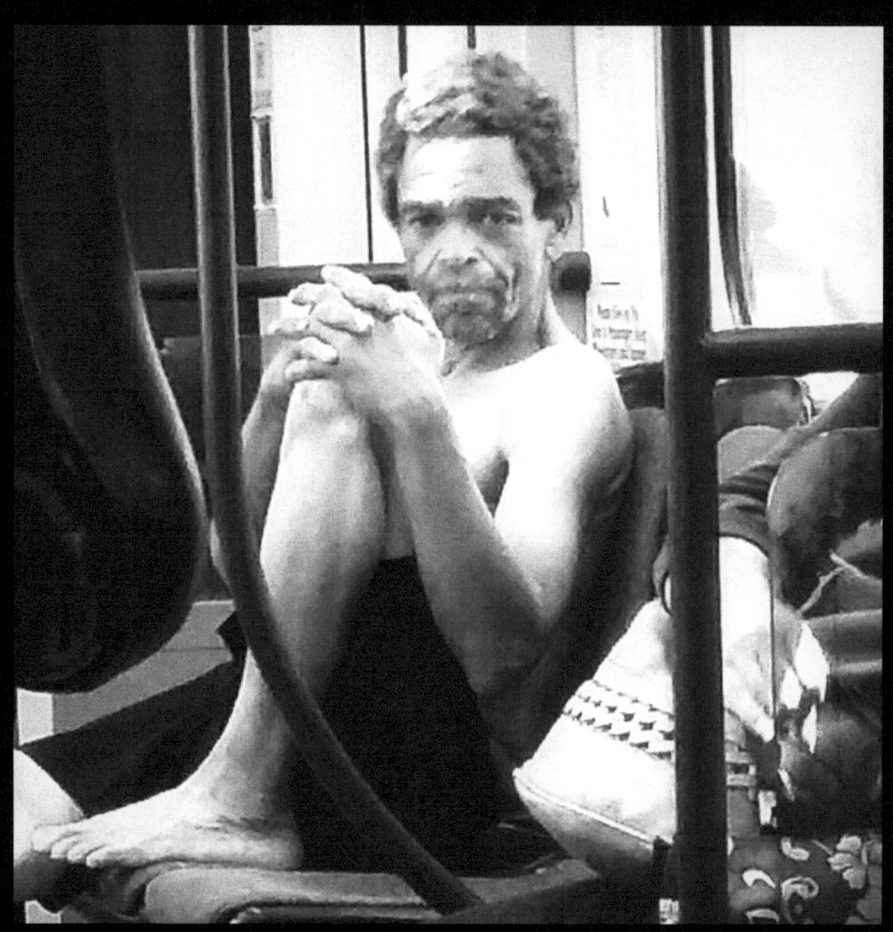

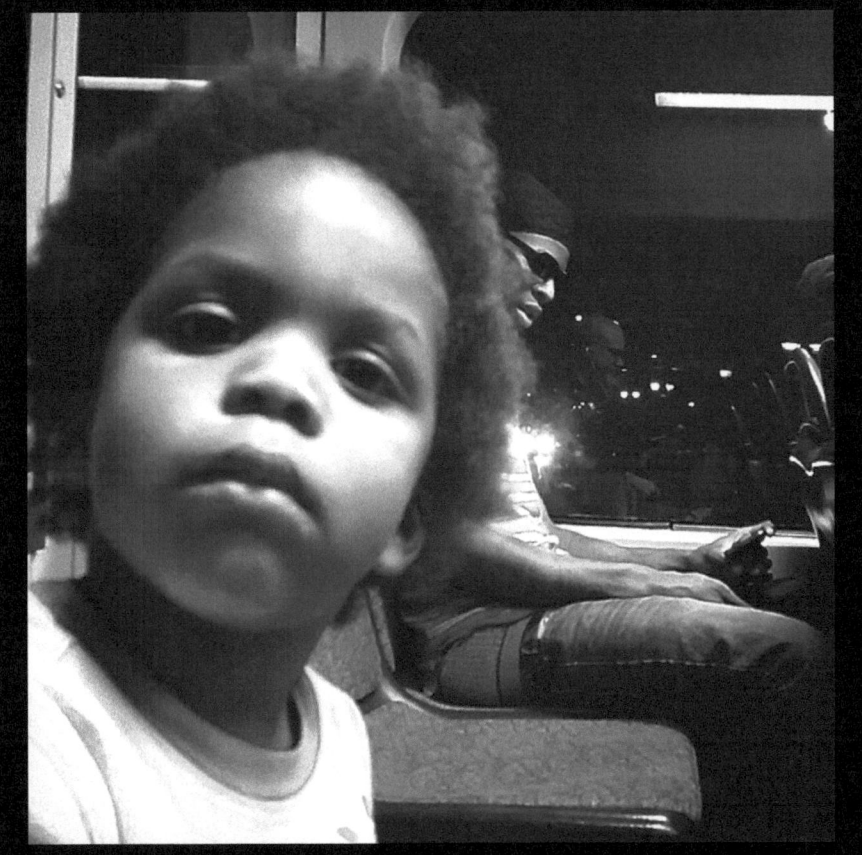

A family got on one evening, and instead of sitting next to his mom, this young man chose to climb up next to me. He never said a word, but he seemed to exude "Whatchu talkin' 'bout?"

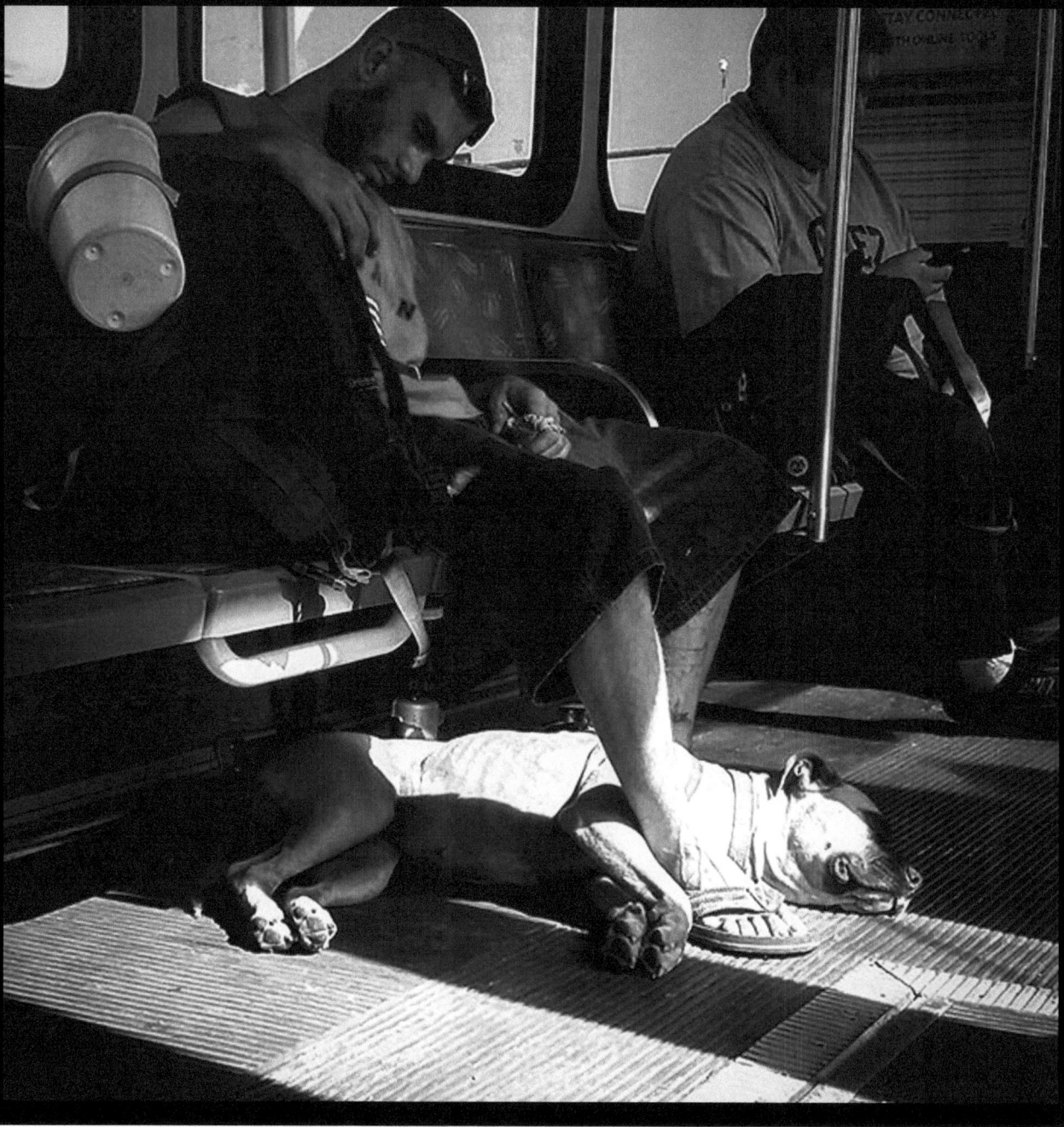

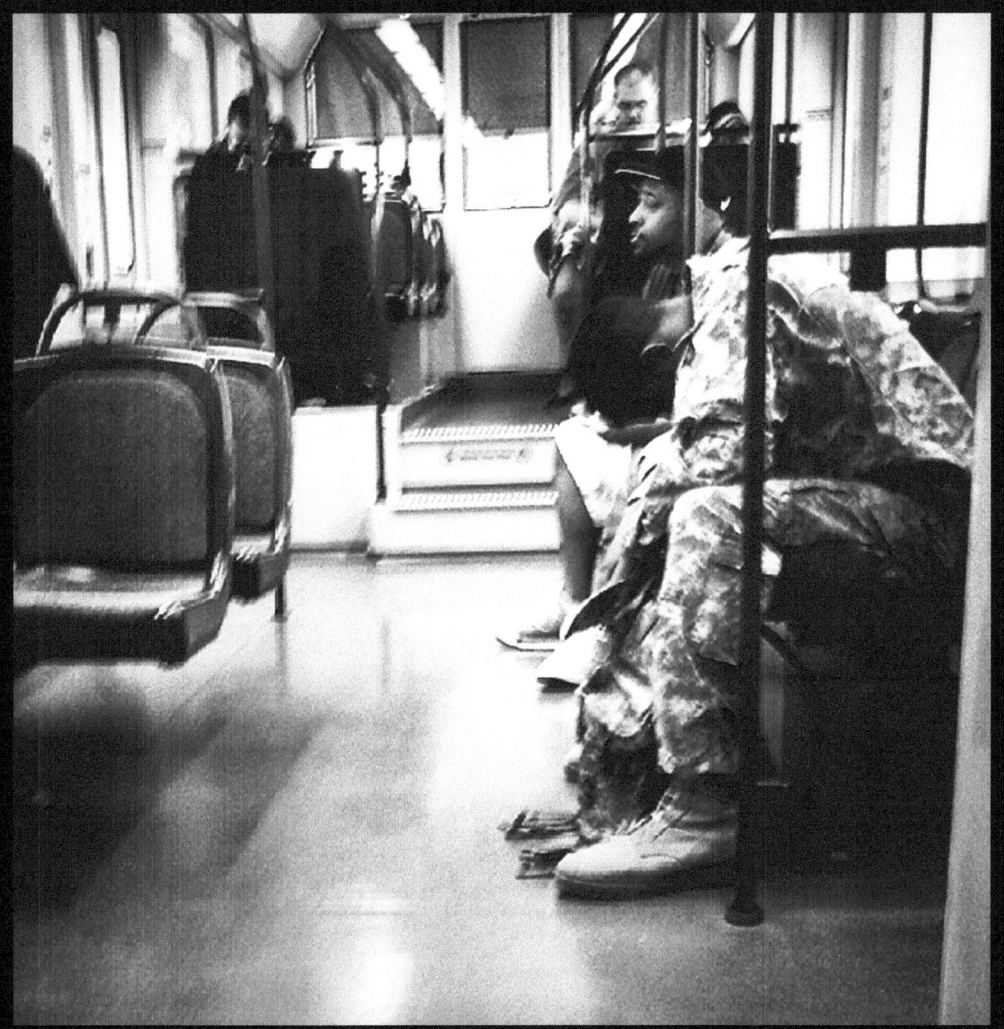

I don't know where this young man was headed, but he seemed to be carrying the weight of the world on his shoulders.

I was ready to call the coroner, or the EMTs.
Then he started snoring. For the next hour.

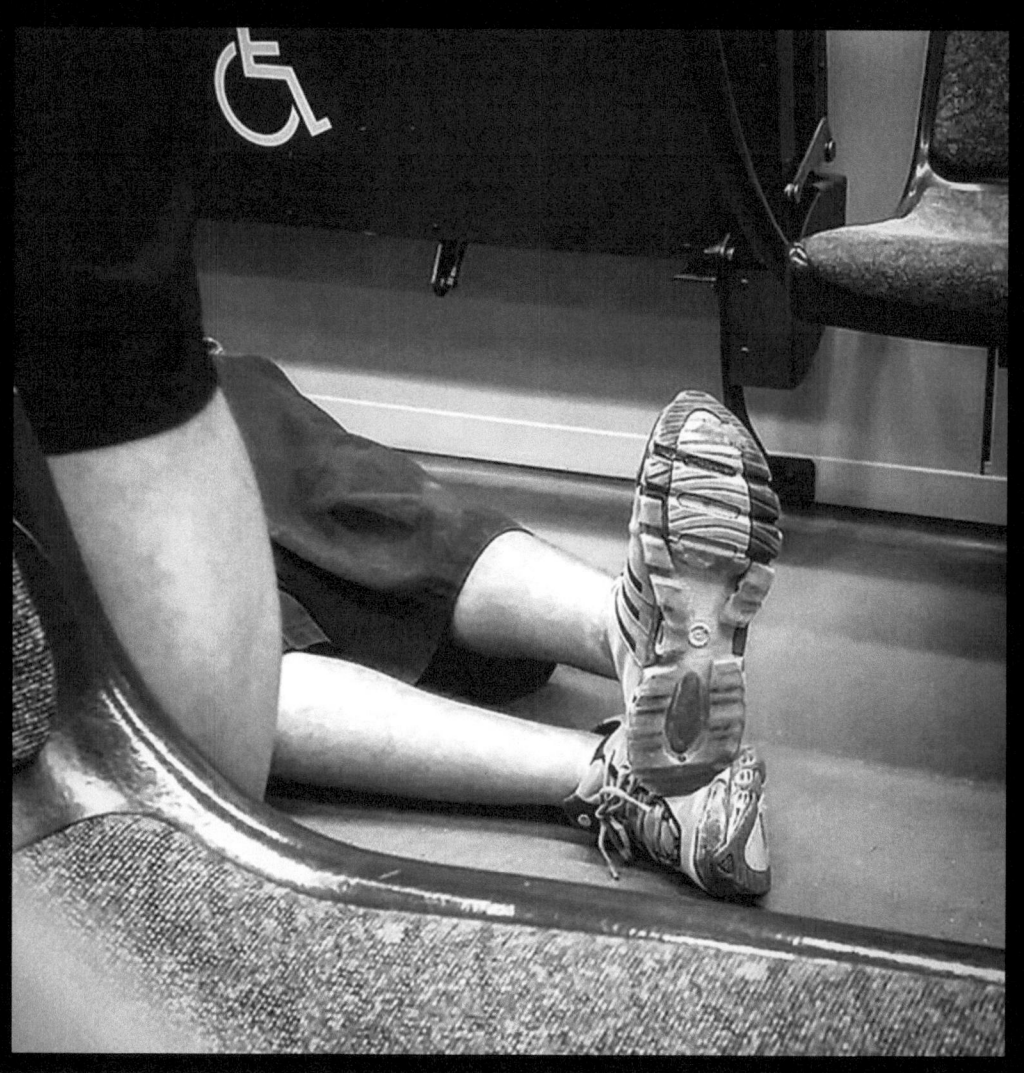

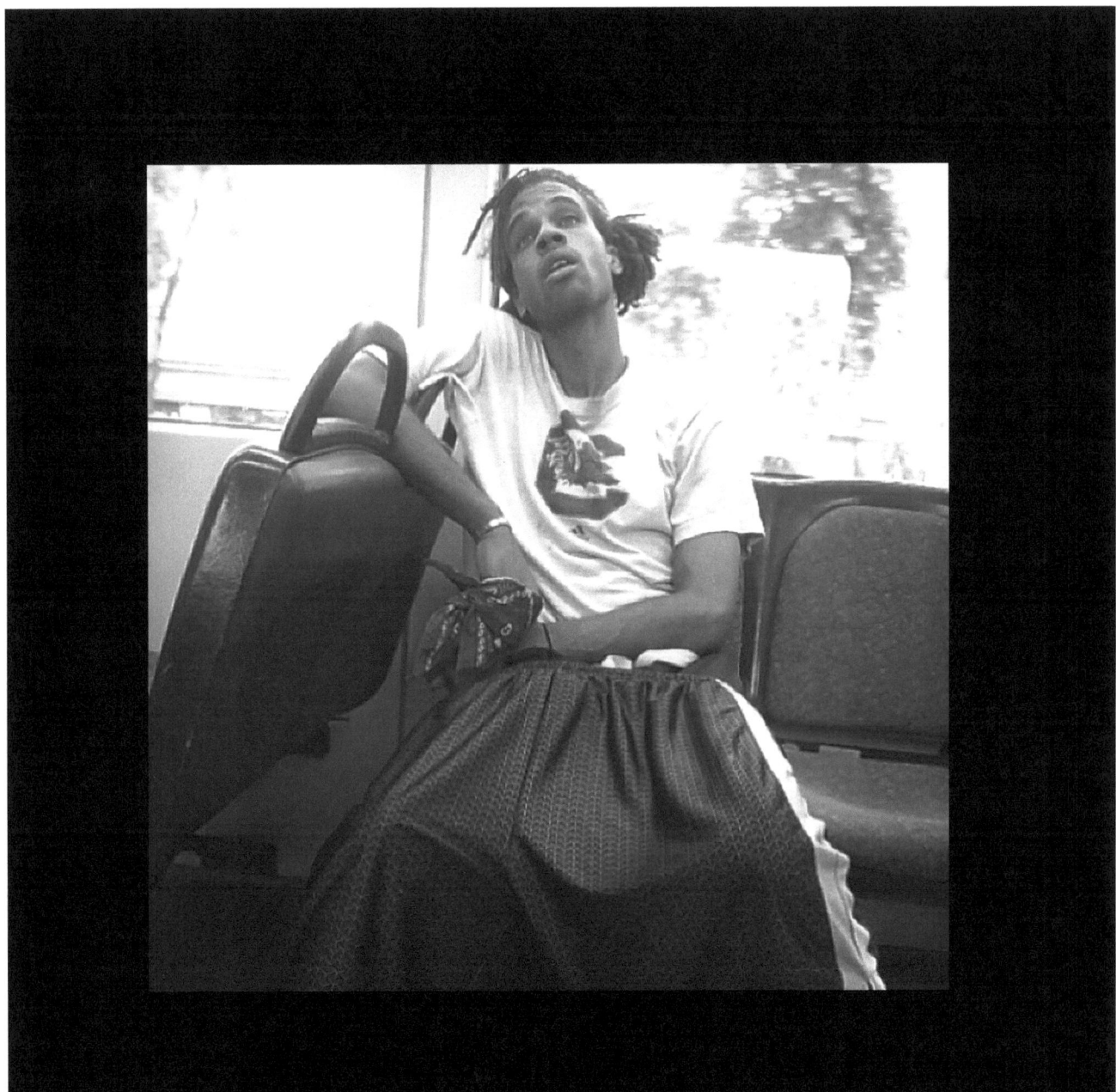

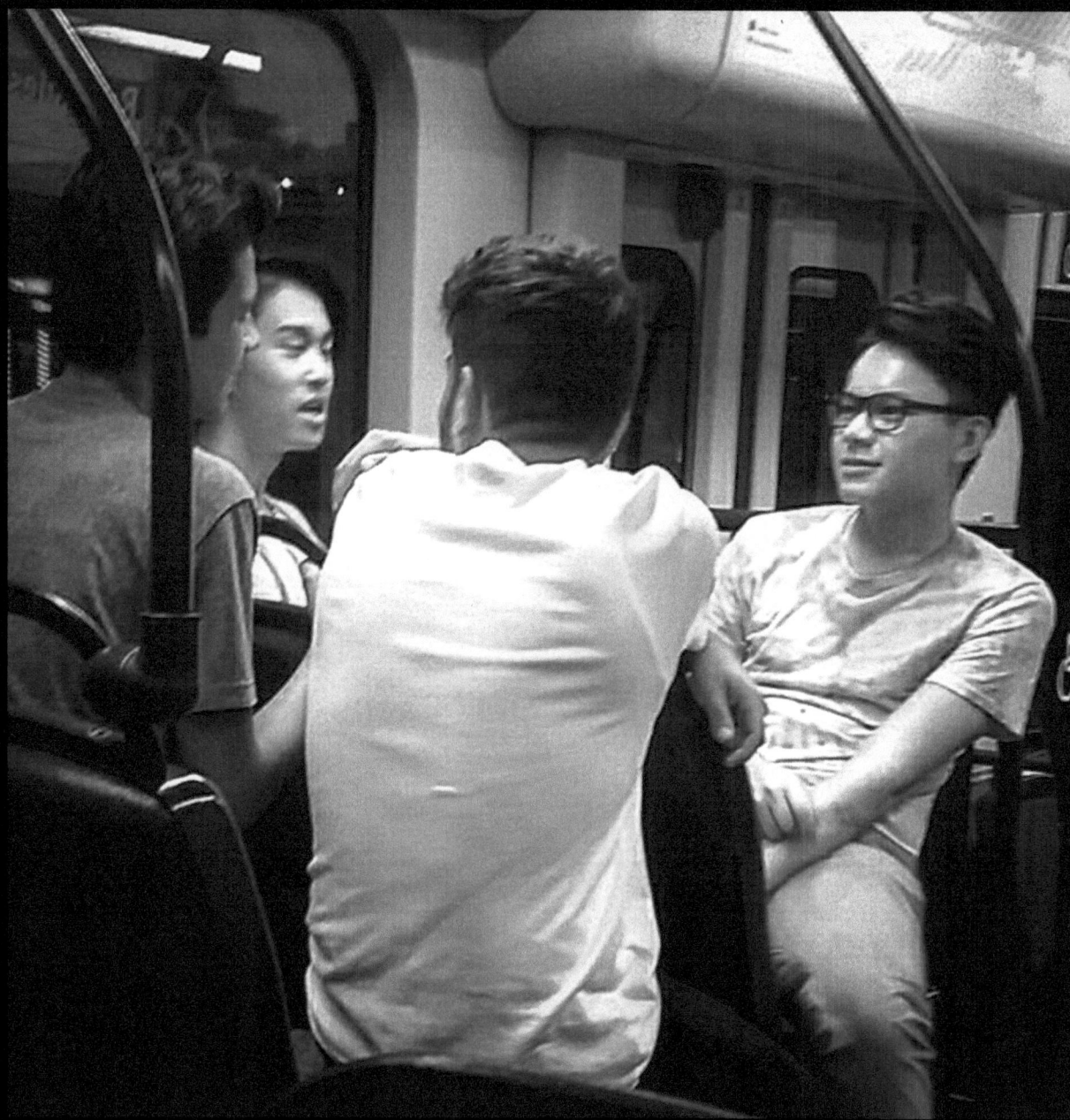

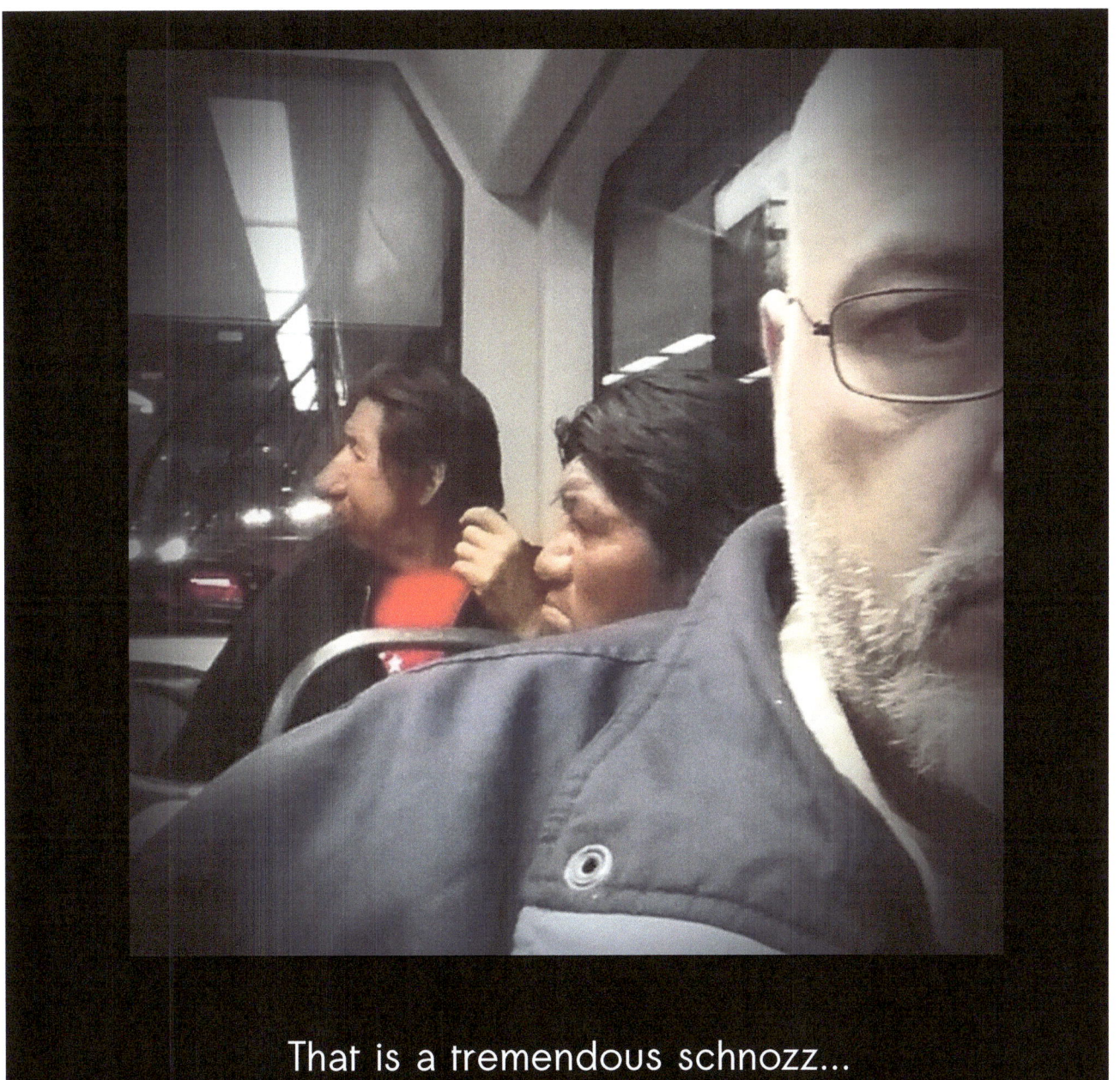

That is a tremendous schnozz...

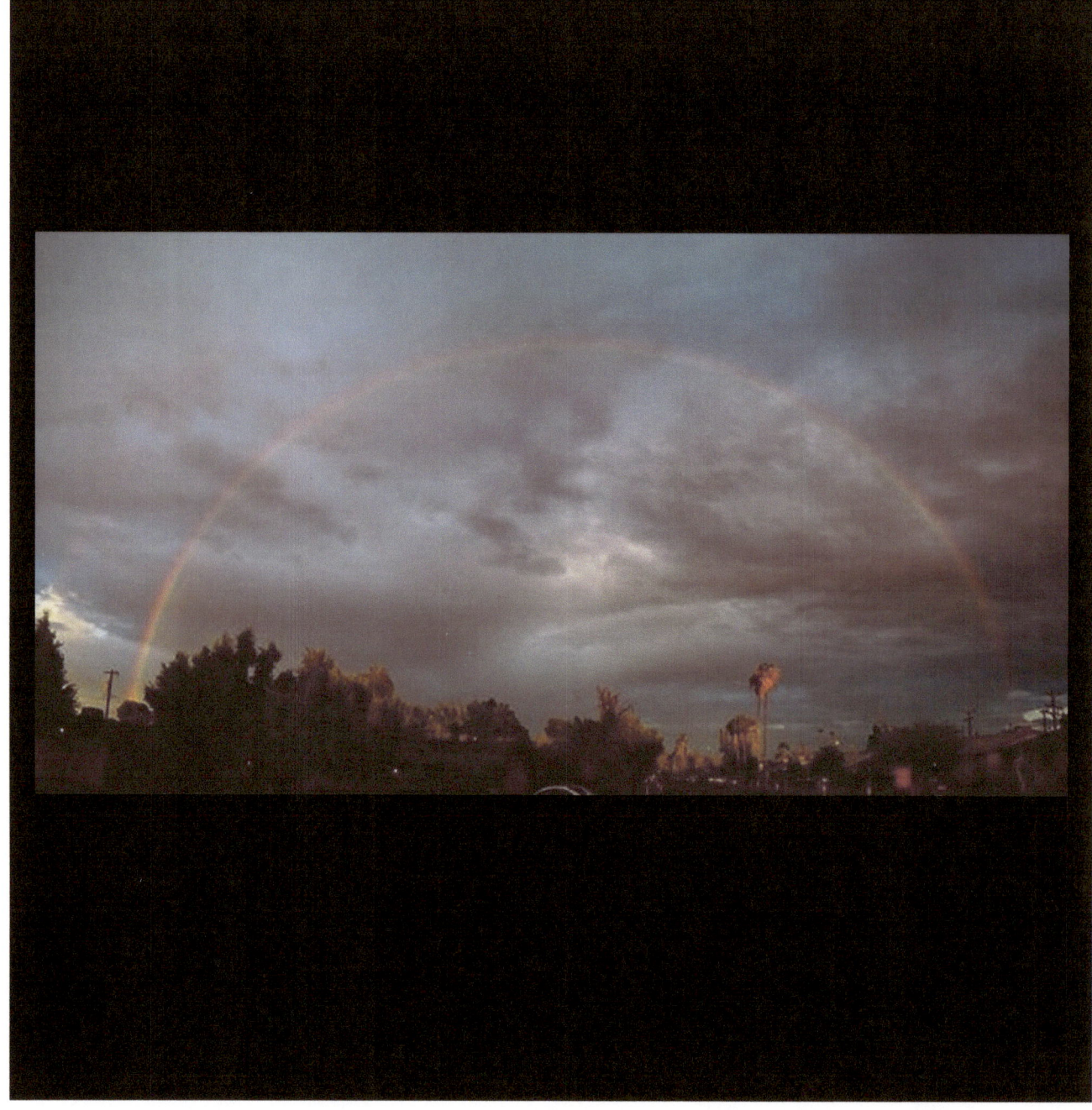